In The Moment
By Rashaun J. Allen

In The Moment Copyright © 2011 by Rashaun J. Allen. Fourth Edition.

Edited by Jan Tramontano

Cover photo by Pavel Yamakov © 123rf.com

Back photo by Sharpshitter © 123rf.com

All rights reserved. No part of this book may be reproduced in any form, except for the inclusion of brief quotations in a review, without permission in writing from the author or publisher.

Published by Royal Blue Publishing

Library of Congress Control Number: 2012909549

ISBN: 978-0-9830096-1-0 (pbk)

ISBN: 978-0-9830996-2-7 (Kindle)

ISBN: 978-0-9830096-6-5 (Epub)

ATTENTION CORPORATIONS, UNIVERSITITES, COLLEGES AND PROFESSIONAL ORGANIZATIONS: Quantity discounts are available on bulk purchases of this book for educational, gift purposes, or as premiums for increasing magazine subscriptions or renewals. Special books or book excerpts can also be created to fit specific needs. For information, please go to www.royalbluepublishing.com

About The Author

Rashaun J. Allen was born in Brooklyn, New York. He graduated with a Bachelor of Science in Business Administration from SUNY Albany and obtained his Master of Business Administration from The College of Saint Rose. He is a brother of Phi Beta Sigma Fraternity Inc. who loves to make a positive impact within the community. He also loves to spend time with his family and friends.

Dedication

To my

Mother, Christine Adina Hunnicutt

and

Grandfather, Charles Edward Hunnicutt Sr.

Acknowledgments

Thank you, Yelena Ramautar for your encouragement. Thank you, Rosaura Elías-Wilson and Amada Gross for reading and sharing your thoughts about earlier versions of this book. Thank you, Jan Tramontano for editing my manuscript. Last but not least, thank you, my supporters and readers.

Also By Rashaun J. Allen

A Walk Through Brooklyn

In The Moment
By Rashaun J. Allen

Table of Contents

Scenes	15
Dream	18
Revolutionary Heart	19
Cost Of Freedom	21
Sharon's Situation	23
Dear Diary	25
Life Like Clyde	26
A Game	27
Tell Her	28
Faithful	29
Foul Play	30
I Knew	31
Sometimes	32
I Miss My Sister	34
Fall Forward	35
Shout Out	36
I Wonder	37
She Drives Me	38
Misunderstood	40
Another Woman	41
Unanswered Questions	42
Man's Best Friend	44
Never Say	45
A Hero	48

Scenes

Staring
in the mirror
"No one will defer my dreams!"
she declared
as she washed her face
she saw visions of herself more clear.
A new life, delivering life
as a wife and obstetrician.
Her position
took persistence
from years of facing her fears
of a broken heart
a promise made
without a promise ring
with care
her heart would be handled.
With a prayer every night
the light shines bright
on her graduation.

Scenes from life aren't black and white
there are shades of gray.
We'll overcome everything.

From the rearview
he has flashbacks
from being the kid his peers used to laugh at.
He couldn't be himself
he was too bright
using big words
he spoke too white.
A superficial
affiliation
led to
a trial of tears.
Separated
from the haters
he stopped reacting
they never made it.
Time flies
acting became love
shout out to the cornball
and the douchebag
"If you never played me, I could never play you,
thank you!"

Scenes from life aren't black and white
there are shades of gray.
We'll overcome everything.

Snap, snap, family portrait
we both said, "I do!"
we can't forfeit
on this highway of love
don't let temporary emotions make permanent
decisions.
With automatic drive on our feelings
we gotta stick shift our opinions
to strive
to work out our differences.
Differences are
money and family
we gotta
build money like a family
and family
can't always see what's best.
Let's beat the odds
for us
the kids
to be in love
for an infinite amount of years.

Scenes from life aren't black and white
there are shades of gray.
We'll overcome everything.

Dream

A dream!
Martin had one
that one day
from marching like an army
to fight racism, the right of liberty
would let freedom ring.
Despite discrimination, despite segregation
shouts of free at last cracked the glass ceiling
from a black man in the white house
to a Latina in the supreme court.
But don't get caught up in the hype
it's a long walk to freedom, we still have a hike.
Look at the plight
jails are built faster than schools.
In Arizona, asking your citizenship status is cool.
If Martin had a dream
why didn't the dream act pass?
How can we claim justice, when our brothers are
killed for being black?
Am I next?
Today, what would Martin say?
To unlock the jails education is key.
Become a storm of protest to appeal discrimination
wherever it appears.
Righteously resist until change occurs.
But what will you do to make it ring true?

Revolutionary Heart

Militant mind
Assata Shakur of our times
if we weren't so deaf
if we weren't so dumb
if we weren't so blind
would you be easy to find?
Could I Google you?
GPS your address?
Find you on Facebook, to send a friend request?
Are you stuck in a time, where clenched fists meet
heavy hearts of anguish?
Fighting for freedom
fighting for rights
fighting for life
failure could cost your life
or buy you death.
Can you tattoo that stress?
Cause our skin color is used
to distinguish, divide, demoralize, deprive
so much so some say the revolution DIED!
The revolution died?
Where's the doctor?
There's still time
revolution fell in cardiac arrest
all we need to do is
pump courage

pump knowledge
pump unity
so when I say shush, be quiet.
We all hear its heart beat loud as a riot.

Cost Of Freedom

I love her
she loves me
between us
we have a child
but we're never together.
I do time
behind bars
talk to her through letters.
Raise my child through visits
it seems like forever
is the next time
I'll see my daughter again.
All I can say
is don't be a child with grown up problems.
Then
it's back to the cell
back to the hell
back against the wall
please, please, pick up your cell.
This phone call is like fresh air.
Living conditions are death here.
So commissary is so necessary.
Don't tell me your next visit
is never-wary.
Cause I'm always hurried.
Did u hear the beep?

Just the thought
next time it clicks
makes me sick.
I'm fighting for my life
the judge on vacation
this lawyer could careless
my case in litigation.
What does freedom cost?

Sharon's Situation

Sharon's thirteen and burning
but I'm not talking 'bout playing with fire
if her Pop found out
he's bound to take me for a liar.
Trapped behind bars imagine his face
learning his daughter is moving faster than his case.
An indescribable feeling
this situation is so frustrating
that the faint of heart
will throw up from aggravation
while we're contemplating
how could this ever happen?
A seventh grader, caught up in a grown up
transaction.
What's the predicament?
Is Mommy always gone?
Wrong!
Are boys always there?
True!
Mommy lets them spend a night in the same room.
What was Mommy thinking?
They too young to think 'bout sex
he too young to think 'bout breast
and Sharon's too smart to ever say yes.
it's not that, Sharon meant to catch feelings
it's just that

truth or dare was appealing.
I dare you
to lift up your skirt
the truth is
if I put it in it will hurt.
If Sharon had even heard of a condom
A STD, may not have been her problem.

Dear Diary

There's nothing new under the sun.
But why did he take my heart and run?
He had choices
we both made decisions.
Now I'm here in a juxtaposition
between a rock and a hard place
to save face
Should I abort our child?
I don't think so but then again
can I do it on my own?
While his Dad just blows in the wind
jumping out on a limb
reflecting, on the nice things he said.
Was it all to get me in bed?
Now I'm hurting, scared and abused
I have to tell Mommy
I hope she knows what to do
but she didn't even notice my tummy getting big
too busy living her second childhood

to pay attention to her kid.

Would she even notice if I disappear?

Grab my bag and my favorite doll

I'm outta here.

Life Like Clyde

Clyde's father couldn't understand
his son was gifted, handsome, and talented
stood out in everything he did.
But he didn't want to claim a misfit
to him, Clyde would only bring shame.
To Clyde, it made sense like a glove fit a hand
he be attracted to a man.
He felt torn
the same day
he came out
was the same day
his father kicked him out.
Left to live in an orphanage
he wished the tissue
used to wipe his face
would erase the issue
of being gay.
With hope in the unseen
it was much more to him
his father would see
he concluded
he'd turn
what was a nightmare
into a livable dream.

A Game

Caught up in the system
with no control, nor someone to console
life ain't a game to these players, pray for 'em.
Reality's *iller* than the graphics
few shoot for the stars, that's tragic!
Survival is the only skill worth mastering.
Vital signs of life, the world's laughing.
The only thought in his mind
 "Am I gonna eat today?"
just hoping, to stay in a place
where love outshines misery.
It's no mystery, living in an orphanage
don't offer kids many options
left to adapt with no continues.

Tell Her

Tell her
how much I care
tell her
how much she means to me
tell her
how much I fear
losing her over a lie, trialed and tried, trumping the truth.
What would I do?
Where would our future go?
Out the door and slammed behind?
Can our love survive the test of time?
I need an answer
to appeal
to my heart
to be patient.

Faithful

Just the thought of being faithful, I lose my breath.
My head hurts. I get pains in my chest.
The union with her is causing unrest, civil war
between my mind and heart.
I ask myself, "Is love hard to find?"
Followed by, "Is she right for me?"
Only time would tell and this time I'd substitute
time for a tattle-tale
No more games, my aim isn't to steal base to score.
I'm here to love you for your flaws and all.
All I ask is for trust and to be honest
I feel like whatever you ask, you ask for more.
Growing pains are pills that we pop together.
We went from strangers, friends, to lovers
and I want what we have to last forever.
My best friend, I will strive to be faithful.

Foul Play

It was my son's game, he came up to bat.
I started yelling from the bleachers, "Hit it out of
the park!"
Another man started screaming, "Go Chris!"
I looked at him, then my son, oh God, say it
couldn't be
like father, like son, he walks and talks like me.
But how the hell does my son look like him?
I wish my eyes lied to my mind
cause at that moment, I could have choked him to
death.
I never want to feel this way inside
ticking like a bomb
any second I'm bound to explode.
What stopped me from losing it?
Was picturing my ex's face when I screamed, "Why
my son ain't mine?"
It never happened, when we locked eyes, I cried.
My heart's on trial
the DNA test confirms we can never be
just like this feeling of hurt is never gonna heal.
How can I walk out of his life like it's no big deal?
Imagine.
I tell him, look son, I'm not your Dad when I'm the
only father he ever had.

I Knew

I knew they didn't like me when I entered.
I couldn't help my smile was so bright.
I knew this moment was my time.
It just felt so right.
I knew my goals weren't easy.
I chose the path less traveled.
Even when few believed, I knew I had a gift.
My dreams are the reality I made exist!

Sometimes

Sometimes when we argue
I wonder if we're really that close.
Sometimes when we fightin'
I wonder if we meant that blow.
Sometimes when we hurtin'
I wonder why we cut so deep.

And if I ever lost you would I lose a part of me?
I hope I never know cause first and foremost
family means the world to me.
I wanna let you know
I'm a work in progress and all things take time to
grow.

Sometimes when we argue
I wonder if we're really that close.
Sometimes when we fightin'
I wonder if we meant that blow.
Sometimes when we hurtin'
I wonder why we cut so deep.

And if you ever need me
I'll be right there by your side
I hope you always know
for the good, the bad and all those ugly times
I wanna let you know
family means more than I could ever show through poetry.

Sometimes when we argue
I wonder if we're really that close.
Sometimes when we fightin'
I wonder if we meant that blow.
Sometimes when we hurtin'
I wonder why we cut so deep.

And would you pick up the phone if I had an emergency?
I really wanna know
my voice will reach you
and your hand will lift me up
so that I never fall.

I Miss My Sister

I'm not in your life the way I want to be.
I miss my sister.
I would change your diapers and push you on the
swings.
I miss my sister.
Why can't life play out the way I want it to be?
I smile reminiscing about
that day I went on a date
you tried to come
grabbed your jacket
and shouted
"Shaun, wait for me!"
I was mad back then
now, I could shed tears
how I miss you.
It's not that you're gone
how I miss you.
It's more like you're far
and my calls can't reach you.
A gift can bring you joy
but a gift can't compare
to how I feel
when I see you.

Fall Forward

When I fall, I fall forward, I never lose my way.
I recited, a poem to a friend.
She said, "You have skills but lack confidence!"
She was blind to the road I walked.
She had no idea, how long I was stuck on Fear Ave,
right by Self-Doubt Boulevard.
The red light became the spotlight
my heart's on display
to my dismay, I lost my first show
but I collected my composure like my poetry
and on the bus home, I swore to a friend
"I would write a book one day!"
That was yesterday
today I have a book, I been on tour and I get calls to
perform on stage.
So forget plan B, fall forward and stay the course of
plan A.

Shout Out

Shout out to my blessings, my worries, and
struggles.
Shout out to the fake friends that swear they love
me.
Shout out to my family, not related by blood
the good life must be created by us.
Shout out to my boss that fired my ass.
Shout out to the cheater that helped me pass.
Shout out to the ho that taught me game.
Shout out to excuses that taught me blame.
Shout out to luck when proper planning prevails.
Shout out to guts having the heart to fail.
Shout out to God those gun shots never touched me
to keep it one hundred, He must love me.

I Wonder

I wonder.
When you stare in the mirror what do you see?

I wonder.
If you know you're beautiful?

You remind me
of the girl that walked into my universe
and became my world
your smile lit up the sky
your tears created water
your touch created life
and as I walked closer
you stole my breath away
hiding your face
your reflection was of a queen
the girl of my dreams

I wonder.
When you stare in the mirror what do you see?

I wonder.
If you know you're beautiful?

She Drives Me

As I
put the key in the ignition
she took the wheel.
"You drove stick before?"
She smirked
"No big deal!"
My eyes widened
speechless
I strapped up.
Thinking.
If she drives how she love, I might get hurt.

She checked the mirrors
just to say
"I'm a bad bitch!"
As she adjusted her seat
I bit my lip.
I signaled her
so she could watch what she was doing.
She ignored
just to rev the engine.
And that's when I knew, she loved her position.

I thought the tank was on E from how slow she moved.
Suddenly she switched gears
moving as fast as a Nascar.
I made her downshift
so the clutch and shifter could work together.
She reversed what she was doing
her driving got better
I couldn't help but sweat her.
The AC didn't help
too much friction on the leather.
She would have claimed I shouted from the jolts in motion
I knew she was open.
We never made it out the parking lot
as we came to a stop.

Misunderstood

I can get any girl in the world.
But once I get her
sharing my feelings is an unexplored island
she travels to unravel a piece of myself.
She's puzzled
I tell her
she's the one
but can't utter my feelings.
I'm a walking contradiction
treating the relationship like a fantasy
it's non-fiction.
We've been talking for a while
she's no longer a joint
and I'm no longer *him* to all her friends.
It's a simple step
just flip the M in me
I guess my confidence isn't as cracked up as it
needs to be.
I'm afraid to be hurt
so instead of being romantic
I come off as a jerk.

Another Woman

You opened your heart like a door.
Catered to me like a chef I adored.
I was a fool like a joker and ashamed.
I treated your heart like a video game.
I wished it was a lie as I try to explain
my stomach bubbled
my throat started to crack.
As I uttered the words
I'm in...
I'm in love with another woman.
It's just that
when I'm with her, I can cure the sick
time stops, I never hear a clock tick.
When I hold her, she's a part of me.
And telling you
is the hardest part for me.
How could I be the one
to break your heart
to make you cry
to make you hate every guy.
What we had was genuine
we had fun, we had trust
and if we had nothing we had us.
I'm sorry, it's not you.
I'm sorry, I chose her.
But I'm glad I decided to tell you.

Unanswered Questions

Why did my boy's cousin land in jail?
He knew the code of the street: *don't ever tell.*
But no one ever said the streets weren't for him.
He was gifted since birth, put a ball in his hand,
he'll make you touch earth.
Projected to make something of himself, his whole
life his family had been foreign to wealth.
All he had to do was stay inbound.
But the streets brought out the worse in him
so he ended up the best baller in jail.

Why did my friend's sister get hit by her lover?
She's a ride-a-die chick, of course she talk slick.
She's strong!
She helped her mother raise her brothers, alone.
If he walked in her shoes then he'd understand her
tone.
That's neither here nor there
but if her brothers find out
I swear it would get ugly.

Why did my old homie lose his new son?
Every decision he made was for his little one.
He knew fatherhood, he stepped up to the plate
when most his peers who had children
left their kin to fate
his son's memory
never forgotten
just like losing hope for brighter days was never a
option.

Man's Best Friend

My owner's relationship from the outside
appears to be a beautiful bliss.
But as her dog
I see what happens behind closed doors
that bruise on her arm is not from a fall
the gifts he buys to cover up the flaws
can never replace years of drama.
She could do so much better
for a word spelled with four letters.
She's fighting back tears
family visits, no need to talk about the weather
his anger's the real blizzard.
I bark to try to tell them
he's more animal than me.
They don't understand
they just tell me to be quiet.
But family matters
so, I'm left to take matters into my own paws
when the yelling gets too loud
her cries go unheard
and he's foreign to reason.
I diplomatically take a dump on the carpet
so when his fist hit flesh
she takes no part in it.

Never Say

Never say never
it can't happen to me.
Who would've thought
never could happen to me.
Having a baby
just like my peers
to me it appeared
they were doing it purposely.
While I accidentally
went raw that one time.
I remember
like it was yesterday
coming back from dinner
you felt you found a winner.
We laughed as we made our way
back to my place
one thing led to another
we flirted
we kissed
became intimate
without a rubber.
We both agreed
nothing would happen.
A silly thought
REALLY!
Nothing could happen?

Cause then
you missed your period.
But a period ends a sentence not begins one
you told me in one ear
you're pregnant
and in the other ear
my selfish thoughts crept in.

You're not even my wife.
You're kinda, sorta my girl.
I have a future to protect
weeping and shouting won't change the pretext.
I swore to keep it real
but I don't even know, how I feel or what I want.
How could I give my world up?
Without a second thought
for our unborn child
Be a father?
What if we don't last?
We talked about a future but our time came and passed.
Can we even keep up with the bills?
We're struggling.
I got two jobs, I'm hustling.
What about your dreams?
You know what happens to a dream deferred.
Adoption's an option, so is abortion.
Would you rather keep our baby?

I can't sleep
we made the decision
to abort our child.
It was our decision
a ref would've called foul.
It was swift and quick like pressing backspace on
the keyboard.
Now she's throwing up and I'm feeling sick.
I would have stayed a kid
to avoid this feeling.
It's like a mental bid
and my heart wants to appeal it.
Sleepwalking through the day seeing images
of how life could have played out.
If you were my son
I could see us shooting hoops.
Or my daughter
I could see us going to the zoo.
As I turn to my girl in bed to share my heartache
I notice her tummy still big
overcome with joy
let's have our kid.

A Hero

A hero in my eyes, a father to me too
the one that picked me up, the one I cried to
who knew you'd survive the struggle
when your wife died, to raise your children
then helped raise their kids
turning your grandchildren into Toy R Us kids.
You didn't speak much but your actions roared
bike rides with you felt like world tours
going to Dad's house was a holiday.
I remember you were upset I planned to travel
faraway.
Smiles on our faces were a part of your plan
remember when you cooked for us
and burnt your hand.
I'm having flashbacks about the good ole days
I guess the good die young
who cares if you were four times my age
the rock of our family
you were awesome in so many ways.

www.ingramcontent.com/pod-product-compliance
Lightning Source LLC
LaVergne TN
LVHW041501070426
835507LV00009B/732